The Whiteboard Effect

Erase the Past and Re-write a Brilliant Future

For my friend Connie,

the originator of the idea for this work

and the source of endless

insight and inspiration.

TABLE OF CONTENTS

A BRIEF INTRODUCTION 7

PUBLISHER'S NOTE: 11

HAPPINESS VS. HELL 15

THE MECHANISM 21

THE ANSWER WITHIN 29

PRACTICE MAKES PERMANENT 35

A CLEAN SLATE 43

IGNORE YOUR THOUGHTS 49

YOU ARE FREE 53

THE PROCESS 59

GRATITUDE 67

BONUS CHAPTER 71

A Brief Introduction

I know. I'm not too fond of introductions myself. So, I'll be brief. *The Whiteboard Effect* outlines various components of being human—our thoughts, emotions, behaviors, actions, and relationships—and how they interact to create positive and negative experiences in our work, home, and interpersonal relationships. This book guides us through understanding how to erase negative messages and re-write positive impressions that can lead to lasting change.

The Whiteboard Effect offers insights into how we can cultivate more self-awareness and apply mindful acceptance practices to develop a healthier relationship with ourselves; and how we can leverage relationships with family, friends, and team members as a source of strength rather than weakness. It provides the means for unlocking the capacity for personal development using simple yet effective strategies.

These insights are independent of any outer circumstance or personal characteristics;

they do not adhere to specific religious or philosophical teaching.

The Whiteboard Effect stands out for its simplicity, effectiveness, and rapidly evident results. The ease of this approach practically disguises the benefit of the procedure. Simply stated, it frees us from the emotional attachments that primarily cause our suffering and hold us back.

Publisher's Note:

Get More Out of This Book

Sterling Sill, author of over 30 books, once wrote about an article he read entitled *How to Get More Out of a Book Than There Is in It.* "Good readers," he explained, "may be able to get out of a book all there is in the book, but with a little imagination and some ability to analyze, they may get much more."

 All capable readers can have their thoughts strike a particular notion, causing their thinking to drift away from the material they are reading. We should not be too quick to draw our minds back into the book, since frequently if we give our imagination a little freedom, it will direct us to some *interrelated* way of thinking that could prove to be extremely valuable.

People may often find that the most significant insights, ideas, and beliefs are the ones that they come up with on their own and not so much from the concepts printed on the page. As our mind wanders along its own specific chain of correlated thought, we may arrive all on our own at some important interpretations and impressive conclusions. Then, when our minds have finished their journey of exploration and discovery, we can return our attention to the book and resume reading.

This is how to get more out of a book than there is in it. The book will cause us to come to conclusions regarding a diversity of *notions not actually in the book*. The interest of freeing our thoughts is an extremely beneficial and rewarding undertaking.

Paul, the New Testament apostle, was a known ponderer. He advises us that "whatsoever things are true, whatsoever things are honest, whatsoever things are just, whatsoever things are pure, whatsoever things are lovely, whatsoever things are of good report . . . *think on these things.*"[1] The ability to ponder gives us the capacity to obtain more from our circumstances and situations than what is actually in them. Through this procedure we place ourselves above the conventional and commonplace existence.

Thousands of fantastic, fascinating philosophies are frittering away in countless books. Hundreds of important and profound programs that could benefit us immensely sit untouched on library shelves. Even the word of God Himself remains largely unfamiliar and unacquainted to many of us. All the essential ingredients for success in any of our personal pursuits cannot advance our progression until we ingest and absorb them; until we get them circulating in our bloodstream and make them a part of our inner strength and learning.

As you read this book, or any other, practice the art of pondering. It will give you a more prolific passion for learning and thinking and, hopefully, for putting into practice. If what you read here does not please and persuade you, so much the better. You can amend each gem or each chapter to your own specific situation to satisfy your own particular prerequisites.

Effective pondering will enable you to draw concrete conclusions and form compelling objectives on the vital subject of your personal progress in life.

Happiness
vs
Hell

Humans were created for happiness, yet many live as if they were passing through hell. They toil away at jobs that don't bring them joy, trying to make enough money to buy things that won't satisfy their deepest desires. They fear taking risks and exploring new possibilities, so instead, they stay in the same patterns of unfulfilling behavior. They want to pull free from the mire that makes their journey to inner peace and happiness arduous and beyond the reach of promising prospects, but they often feel stuck. The harder they pull to free themselves from the sludge of daily living, the deeper they sink into it.

Your capacity for empathy allows you to recognize pain in yourself and others when faced with tough times or difficult situations. These feelings can make you frustrated or angry when your needs are unmet. Similarly, feelings of loneliness or depression can cause you to lose hope. Ultimately this leads some individuals down a dark path of violence or hatred towards themselves or another person as a way of expressing their inner turmoil.

You've probably said, *"There has got to be a better way!"*

Quality of life depends, for the most part, on your attitude. Peace, happiness, joy, love, and success are all intrinsic to the human experience. Yet alongside these positive emotions lies the darker side of humanity—anger, sadness, despair, and hatred. Even though peace and love are more desirable than chaos and violence, the latter elements are also part of what it means to be human.

Humans are creatures of habit. Your habits dictate how you respond to certain situations and influences but can sometimes limit you from achieving your peak performance or reaching your goals. You prefer to stick with what you know; it is comfortable, familiar, and safe. Over time these habits become ingrained, so you need to remain aware that it is acceptable to vary the routine occasionally to achieve the results you desire for yourself, your family, your team, or your company. It is essential to recognize when a habit is holding you back instead of pushing you forward so that you can make changes accordingly.

To enjoy a high quality of living requires developing and maintaining a positive attitude and outlook. The primary question becomes, how do you positively approach life and life's many challenges?

The answer lies in the concept of a simple classroom device known as a whiteboard. *The Whiteboard Effect* is a pragmatic system of eliminating obstacles and attachments and creating new possibilities. It is relevant to our entire life journey: from personal development to healing relationships, from improved classroom performance to enhanced work practices, from erasing past resentments to planning a purposeful and brilliant future—one day at a time.

Is there a way to wipe away the sludge of past emotions and experiences and start again? Despite what happened yesterday, can you let go of the hurt and pain that often accompanies you into the present? Can you rise above competitive resentments, relationship jealousies, and self-criticism? It is possible to heal from life's traumas and toxic situations and live with greater joy, peace, freedom, and purpose.

The self-concept is one of the most insightful discoveries in the history of the social sciences. The self-concept develops over a person's life and shapes their personality afterward. Among the most influential discoveries in the self-concept is that of self-esteem.

Convinced that you had worth as a person from birth, you began to develop a wide range of beliefs about yourself. The self-concept became the master program of your subconscious mind, determining everything you think, say, feel, and do. What you are today is the result of this early conditioning.

No matter where you are in life, happy or hateful, in Heaven or hell, *The Whiteboard Effect* will make your next step clear.

The Mechanism

A whiteboard (dry-erase board, dry-wipe board, or pen-board) is a smooth, glossy, usually white surface for making non-permanent markings. Whiteboards are analogous to blackboards but with a smoother surface allowing for rapid marking and erasing. Whiteboards have become fixtures in many offices, meeting rooms, classrooms, and other work environments. The term whiteboard also refers to interactive whiteboards and 'virtual tech whiteboards.'

Traditional whiteboards require two essential tools:
- a whiteboard maker (or pen) and
- a whiteboard eraser.

The whiteboard pen or dry-erase marker is a non-permanent marker that uses erasable ink. It adheres to the smooth writing surface without binding to it or being absorbed. The whiteboard eraser removes marks quickly and easily, allowing you to move forward promptly.

The concept of the 'tabula rasa' or 'blank slate' theory suggests that you enter the world with no preconceived notions or ideas. Everything you think and feel you learned in childhood. Your mind is like a blank whiteboard on which every experience and each event you have gone through are written. You are the sum of the knowledge you have gained because you are the sum of all you have read, felt, and experienced.

When you believe something, that idea becomes true for you, no matter the reality. Everything you are today results from a longstanding concept or belief that you accepted and held onto throughout your life. All your views, values, opinions, feelings, and attitudes today are built on the concept you developed as a child.

As an example: If you were raised believing that the 1969 moon landing was faked, you may tend to be distrustful of the media and the government. You may see conspiracies and cover-ups, even where none exist. On the other hand, if you were raised believing that Neil Armstrong did set foot on the moon, you may tend to believe in human possibility and in achieving the unachievable. In either case, you were not part of the Apollo 11 crew and cannot personally verify the facts of that venture, and yet, your opinions about it may shape your characteristics.

These deep-rooted beliefs are causing undue difficulties in your life. Your current thoughts are blocking your progression and preventing you from directing your life in a healthier manner. It feels safer to have things easy.

Letting negative thoughts spread into your mind is comparable to poisoning your drinking water. It is harmful and deadly. Consider that **the largest ocean cannot sink even the smallest ship unless the water gets inside it.** When weak, damaging, destroying thoughts get into your mind, you begin to sink fast. It is mental suicide. What if you could use the mechanism of the whiteboard to erase the hurt feelings and mistakes of the past and begin each day with a clean, blank slate? And what if you could use that mechanism in the very moment when negative emotions disrupt your daily performance?

"If you form a picture in your mind of what you would like to be, and you keep and hold that picture there long enough, you will soon become exactly as you have been thinking." - William James

The Whiteboard Effect opens a pathway for anyone willing to travel that route. You will improve your life if you apply the principles described in this book. They are easy to understand and implement and will not cost you a dime. Research has indicated that this approach is more effective in relieving negative psychological responses than many of its counterparts.

All outward change occurs when you change your inner perceptions. Your world changes when you change how you think and feel about yourself and the world in which you live. The primary requirement for *The Whiteboard Effect* to work is a willingness to erase your habitual belief systems and any current negative attachment to work, family, or life experience.

The subconscious mind is, in effect, a whiteboard with some of the same issues all whiteboards have. You receive many constant mental impressions-these impressions become written on your subconscious mind like markings on a once-clean whiteboard. Some of these impressions are positive, and many of these markings are negative. A mental impression on the subconscious can be any effect, feeling, or image retained because of experience, like flying in an airplane for the first time. It can also be a vague notion, remembrance, or belief, like the impression of having met someone before.

In both cases, pressure produces a mark on the smooth surface. The more pressure exuded on the surface, the more permanent the impression. You and everyone in your life have been writing on your whiteboard, and it has recorded all messages written on it without any bias. The whiteboard does not discriminate between truth and lies, criticism and praise, helpful information and junk.

Your whiteboard registers everything!

The Whiteboard Effect is the perfect tool for erasing the negative impressions written on the subconscious mind, giving you a clean slate for the positive, loving images that will dramatically alter your world for the better. By applying these methods, you can access internal stores of resilience and prosperity, allowing you to make significant progress toward meaningful goals and objectives. It offers a process for uncovering and utilizing your untapped potential to achieve greater levels of happiness, unconditional love, success, inner peace, and overall well-being.

The Answer
Within

One obstacle to happiness is the conviction that it's not attainable. This perception often becomes embedded, keeping you from even attempting to find happiness. You become convinced that absolute joy comes with a catch. You may think it's too good to be true, or you may think it is only feasible for other individuals; *your* life is more complicated.

You're easily upset. You get angry. Maybe you're discouraged or depressed. You feel like life is an endless struggle that leads nowhere but to the grave.

You look for relief.

You take anger management classes, or maybe you see a therapist. You get religion, balance your chakras, meditate, take tranquilizers, become vegan, or take up exercising.

Maybe you discover NLP or start using subliminal suggestion tapes. You have your palm read. You attempt hypnotic regression. You try acupuncture.

Or you throw yourself into endless varieties of psychotherapy.

There is a much simpler way to reach complete clarity, transcending life's problems as you do. It's not about discovering the correct answers or the secret solutions to a magical life; it's about erasing the basis of your problems and re-writing the outcome. The answers are already within you. They are easy to uncover. The process is simple and practical, and it works in everyday life.

You cannot force your way to happiness. Struggle and joy are diametrically opposed. You must cultivate a path of contentment to experience true joy. When you reject the possibility of experiencing joy and pleasure, you unintentionally hold yourself back from reaching your full potential in life. You must erase limiting thoughts and feelings to re-write your dreams and go after what you truly want.

It is the sway of feelings that creates thoughts. Thoughts on their own are painless, but not the feelings that underlie them. One emotion, for instance, can create and re-create thousands of thoughts over time.

Consider one painful memory from the past, such as when you did something you know you shouldn't have done, followed by a bitter regret you've kept concealed. Look at the years of ruminations attached to that single cause. If you could erase the painful feelings associated with that event and surrender the underlying painful feeling, all those thoughts would disappear instantaneously, and you could forget the event.
Thoughts remain filed and stored in the memory bank according to the various shades of feelings associated with those thoughts. Therefore, when you erase or relinquish an emotion, you free yourself from all the associated beliefs. The great

benefit of knowing how to wipe away negative emotions is the capability to do so at any moment and in any place, and it can be done continuously and effortlessly.

Practice
Makes
Permanent

You've undoubtedly heard the expression: 'Practice makes perfect.' The statement isn't exactly true, however. A more accurate hypothesis would be: 'Practice makes permanent.' Suppose you practice riding your bike, dancing ballet, or shooting hoops in a faulty, imperfect fashion. Or perhaps your accounting, marketing, or teamwork efforts are unsound. In that case, you will continue to perform those activities in a flawed, defective manner. Practicing this way will result in a permanently poor performance and not a perfect one.

My first personal computer was a Microsoft product, and I became very proficient at knowing and operating that system. Many years later, I switched to an Apple product. I had to restart the entire computer learning process. I had to unlearn old steps and programs and learn several new ones.

This experience taught me that information written and repeated on the whiteboard of the subconscious can be extremely difficult to erase later in life. This is why bad habits are so difficult to break—physical as well as mental habits.

But the information written there is erasable! It requires effort, but it is possible.

Promptly erasing an office whiteboard will restore its cleanliness and having it look new again. The process is relatively easy. If you clean an office whiteboard frequently, you'll get years of use from this practical, erasable tool. But whiteboards have one major drawback: Frequent use results in surfaces marked with lines and colors that won't easily rub off. The longer the writing remains on the whiteboard, the harder it becomes to remove. It may require a cleaning product like soap or alcohol, a clean cloth, and some much-needed elbow grease.

With a little effort and the proper means, the subconscious mind's whiteboard can also become and be kept clean and like new. The sooner you wipe a negative emotion from your clean slate, the easier it is to remove. The mind learns best through repetition. Suppose similar messages are written on your whiteboard. In that case, the information becomes etched into the smooth surface. It becomes harder to erase, leaving a 'shadow' of negative emotions still visible.

If you write "I am not good enough" on your whiteboard and continue to overwrite on top of it, the bolder the text becomes and the harder it is to erase.

"I'm not good enough… to be financially free."

"I'm not good enough… to be a team leader."

"I'm not good enough… to be healthy and strong."

"I'm not good enough… to be in a loving relationship,"

"I'm not good enough… to be truly happy."

I could fill this entire eBook with examples.

But here's the thing:

Your beliefs are only valid if you believe them.

Please read that again and take the time to process it. **Your beliefs are only valid if *you* believe them.**

You carry an overwhelming reservoir of accumulated negative feelings, attitudes, and beliefs within you. The accumulated pressure makes you unhappy and can become the basis for many diseases and disorders. Most people are resigned to this fact and explain it away as human nature.

Erasing the negativity from your whiteboard is like dropping a hefty weight. It creates a sudden feeling of relief and liveliness. It increases your happiness and your feelings of freedom. It is a simple mechanism of the mind.

You are about to completely erase your limitations and re-write a brand-new life characterized by frequent successes, win-win scenarios, motivation, inspiration, love, happiness, freedom from resentment, creative expression, and thankfulness for everything you've gone through in life.

"As you sow in your subconscious mind, so shall you reap in your body and environment." - Joseph Murphy

Surrendering your feelings can be a complex process. You may be used to holding on to your emotions, making it difficult to let them go. The sense of powerlessness can be overwhelming and may lead you to question why you should surrender these emotions at all. It is important to learn to remove the negative residue of your emotions whiteboard before they become a more permanent mark on your subconscious—your whiteboard. The timelier the erasure, the less effort it will require to remove the writing.

The tendency towards clinging onto emotions often comes from the fear that if you erase them, nothing will take their place or bring you solace. However, erasing your negative emotions creates space for more positive ones, such as happiness and contentment.

A Clean Slate

What is a clean slate—a 'tabula rasa?' It is freedom from negative feelings in any given area, allowing creativity, spontaneity, and joy to manifest without opposition or the interference of inner conflicts.

Being free of internal conflict and expectations allows you to experience the pure and simple nature of the universe, which, you will learn, is that **you can achieve the greatest good in any given circumstance.** This statement may sound merely philosophical, but when accomplished, it becomes true.

You will become:
- more prized for your performance,
- more creative in your committees,
- more trusted by your teams,
- more effective in your employment,
- more respected in your relationships, and
- more affectionate with your family.

Stress is a subject of much attention and publicity. People are more stress-prone than ever. Surprisingly, the natural source of stress is internal, not external. For instance, your propensity to react in anger depends on how much anger waiting within you is ready to be triggered by an outside stimulus. The more offense you have on the inside, the more your perception of the world is one of anger and antagonism.

What you hold inside colors your world.

To the fearful person, this world is a terrifying, frightening place. To the angry person, it is a chaotic and frustrating place. To the guilty person, this world is rife with inescapable temptations and overcome by evil. When you let go of guilt, you can see innocence. The basic rule is: You focus on what you repress.

The rationalizing mind uses projection to suppress the true causes of emotion. It blames events or other people for 'causing' your feelings and views itself as the helpless and innocent victim of external causes.

"The boss made me angry."
"My wife upset me."
"The noise scared me."
"Business meetings cause my anxiety."

The opposite is true. The suppressed and repressed feelings seek an outlet and utilize these events as motivations and excuses to vent themselves. People are like pressure cookers, ready to release steam when the opportunity arises. Their triggers are set and ready to go off.

Because of social conditioning, people often suppress and repress their positive feelings. Suppressed love results in the wounded, broken heart of a heart attack. Hidden love reemerges as excessive adoration of pets, property, and various forms of idolatry. True love is free of fear and characterized by non-attachment. The fear of loss energizes undue attachment and possessiveness.

These psychological vibrations affect human energy systems and reveal effects that can be seen, felt, and measured.

The high frequency of your emotions influences your life experiences on a psychic level. It determines the people whom you allow close to you. Repressed emotions on a psychic level can influence life events. The basic rule of the psychic universe is that like attracts like. Anger is bound to bring about angry thoughts, and love is responsible for love. Loving thoughts, events, people, and pets surround the person who has overcome internal negativity.

Clearing your whiteboard entails acknowledging that a particular emotion exists within you, then allowing it to come up, sticking with it, and letting it run its course without wanting to change it or do anything about it. It means you allow the writing on your whiteboard to exist without focusing on the energy built up behind it.

Allow yourself to experience the feeling without condemning yourself for it or reacting adversely to it. Allow yourself to experience the emotion without being distracted from it, ignoring it, fearing it, condemning it, or moralizing about it. Drop all judgment and understand that it is merely a feeling, simply a word written on a whiteboard. It can easily be removed when you are ready.

Ignore Your
Thoughts

The idea is to experience the writing on the whiteboard (the emotion) without feeling the need to modify it in any way. You may, at first, notice that you feel guilt over having certain feelings. You'll want to wipe them off your whiteboard without examining them first. It will be easier to erase any emotional reaction once you acknowledge that the emotion is there. Observe only the actual feeling rather than the endless, self-supporting thoughts it produces. Thoughts are false, deceitful fantasies that create a wrong picture of the facts.

Pursuing thoughts can keep you occupied endlessly. Eventually, you will learn that you are back where you started. Your thoughts are just rationalizations of the mind to explain the presence of a feeling, and they will only breed more thoughts. A single emotion can replace thousands and even millions of thoughts. Emotions generate thoughts and, eventually, emotions become shorthand for thoughts.

Human instinct requires the survival of self. The mind is a survival mechanism, and emotions mark its method of survival.

Erasing your whiteboard of negative feelings will be the undoing of the ego. Your ego will resist. It will create skepticism about the technique, forgetfulness to follow through with the method, or the venting of negative emotions.

The solution is simply to erase the inscribed emotions. If resistance exists, allow the resistance to be there; don't resist the resistance.

You Are
Free

Erasing your whiteboard is a natural ability. You are making use of your innate capabilities to become freer and happier. You are removing the behaviors which have enslaved and victimized you. These behaviors have blinded you to the truth of your real identity. In time, erasing your whiteboard will become second nature to you. You will no longer think twice before erasing a negative emotion from your subconscious mind. You may find yourself reaching for the eraser without any conscious thought of doing so.

Having a clean whiteboard means you have no emotional attachment to an outcome: it's okay if it happens, and it's also okay if it doesn't. Freedom is letting go of attachments. You can enjoy something, but it doesn't become a requirement for your happiness. There is a progressive diminishing of dependence on anything or anyone outside of yourself.

You're not obligated to erase your whiteboard. You are free to leave your whiteboard undisturbed. No one is insisting you erase it. If you are worried about wiping away a familiar, trusted feeling, examine the fear behind the resistance.

What is the cause of your hesitation in erasing your old thoughts and feelings?

Are you willing to erase these excuses along with the feelings?

Keep erasing each fear as it emerges, and the fear will disappear.

Feelings come and go. Eventually, you will realize that you are not your feelings but merely a witness to them. Your identity is not your emotional state. Your thoughts or your emotions do not change you. By becoming aware of the changeless witness within, you progressively become the primary observer of your feelings rather than the victim enslaved by emotional phenomena.

At times you may feel stuck with a particular emotion. Simply surrender to the feeling of being stuck. Just let it be there, and don't resist it.

Sometimes you may erase a feeling only to notice that the mark is more indelible than you first thought. You erase, but the 'shadow' of what is written on your whiteboard remains. A part of the feeling persists. Some emotions may have been written and re-written, marked with so much pressure and energy, the feeling never entirely disappears from the whiteboard.

Like the words on a whiteboard, some emotions will need a little more time and effort to erase. Still, they will eventually disappear with the right (cleaning) solution. If what is written doesn't fade, erase parts of the feeling in bits and pieces. When tools alone seem insufficient, look to something grander than the self for guidance. Listen to your inner voice for guidance and direction. Allow the light from within to illuminate your pathway.

When your whiteboard is wiped clean, and your mind and heart have once again become a 'tabula rasa,' a blank slate, you will experience a lighter, happier feeling, like an emotional exhilaration. You can remain in that state of happiness and freedom by continuously wiping clean your whiteboard in a timely manner. You will grow closer to your true self and begin to see that you have been duped by your feelings all along. You were the victim of your feelings, but now you know that they do not reveal the truth about you. They are merely thoughtless scribblings your mind mistakenly believed were necessary for survival.

The results of erasing your whiteboard are deceptively quick and subtle, but the effects are potent and powerful.

The Process

All thoughts are filed in the mind's memory bank under a filing system based on the attendant feeling and its finer nuances. They are filed by the tone of the emotion and not by the facts surrounding the sentiment. Self-awareness increases more through the observation of feelings rather than thoughts. Observing your underlying emotions is more rewarding, revealing, and less time-consuming than dealing with your thoughts.

Imagine being approached by a co-worker, classmate, or simply a friend. They say something to you that is thoughtless, unkind, critical, or rude. Suddenly, you notice an emotion rising within you, a word being written on your whiteboard. It could be 'anger,' 'resentment,' 'jealousy,' 'fear,' or any of the myriad negative emotions. Thoughts begin to appear on your whiteboard alongside the feeling. These negative concepts start to 'cloud your whiteboard', filling the free space with negative notions and opinions about yourself.

You begin to wipe away the negative thoughts, but they continue to appear in different idioms and jargon. You can't seem to keep them off your whiteboard. Then you notice the inscribed emotion. You realize that it is that single feeling that is producing all your negative thinking. You acknowledge that feeling, then you take your dry eraser in hand and wipe the emotion off your whiteboard.

Suddenly, the thoughts dissipate and disappear. If one returns now, you simply wipe it away again and move on. Your feelings no longer control you. **You are not the victim of your emotions; you are their master.**

You are free—free to be happy, free to feel joy, free to be who you truly are.

The next time you encounter the offending individual, you will not be burdened by weighty, negative sensations. If a harmful feeling appears on your whiteboard again, you simply dry-erase it away. This will help create harmony in the home and peace in the workplace. Rather than being at odds with others, you will work with unity of purpose.

You choose whether to hang on or let go of emotional upsets.

A part of you may want to cling to a favorite negative emotion. Humans can be mean, selfish, competitive, devious, mistrusting, spiteful, judgmental, malicious, weak, and vain. These emotions are depleting and debasing and create diminished self-respect. They create self-hatred and unending guilt. They seek punishment and disease, yet they are often the feelings most people want to energize and identify with.

Is that how you see yourself? If that's how you see yourself, then that is how others will also see you—your family, your friends, and your co-workers.

What is the cost of hanging on? Do you want to pay that price? Are you willing to accept the feelings?

What are the benefits of hanging on to them? What are the benefits of erasing them?

The choice you make will determine your future. What kind of future do you want?

You can choose to be healed, or you can choose to remain hurt and wounded.

The Whiteboard Effect boils down to the following essential points:
1. Become aware of what you are buying into and what you accept daily.
2. Look at what you have already been programmed with and begin to question it, disassemble it, and erase it.
3. Wake up and free yourself from being exploited and enslaved by the negative programming of the world. You can accept it for what it is—an attempt by others to control you, manipulate you, extract your money, your services, your energy, your loyalties, and capture your mind.

The emotional growth you experience depends on the consistency with which your negative feelings are erased from your whiteboard. Repressed and suppressed feelings require constant energy to keep them submerged. It takes effort to hold down emotions. As the whiteboard is erased clean of negativity, the power that retains the negative feeling is freed up for positive use. Erasing the whiteboard increases available energy for creativity, growth, work, and interpersonal relationships. Pleasure and joy from these activities also improve.

Erasing negative emotions from your whiteboard brings a revitalized sense of well-being and personal growth. You will see joy and pleasure as you start to see the positive results of removing all the roadblocks to success and satisfaction in your life. Happiness and fulfillment will gloriously grow as you begin to make positive changes in your life. Pride and enjoyment will follow as you discover the numerous benefits of ridding your psyche of the impediments to success.

Within a short time, you will discover that your limiting thoughts and negative beliefs, which you once naively held to be accurate, were merely the product of accumulated negative emotion. When the negative feeling is erased, then your thought pattern changes from negative to positive, from 'I can't' to 'I'm happy to.' New areas of your life will open. What once was awkward and pent-up will be effortless and joyful.

Gratitude

Every challenge is a valuable tool helping you to develop your resilience, character, and ambition. Every opportunity presents you with experiences that allow you to push yourself out of your comfort zone and reach higher goals than you may have ever imagined possible.

The tools these challenges and opportunities give are invaluable; they arm you with confidence and skills that cannot be taught in a classroom or through books alone. They help shape how you interact with others as well as how you approach problem-solving in any situation. Embracing an attitude of gratitude towards challenges and opportunities will help you keep perspective during difficult times, allowing for more constructive responses rather than destructive ones.

"Gratitude is one of the deepest expressions of love and there is always something to be grateful for."

Your potential is infinite. It is true that 'you can count the seeds in an apple, but you can't count the apples in a seed.' One seed sprouts and blossoms and then creates many more seeds which, in turn, all sprout, blossom, and create more seeds. Your emotions and thoughts are like seeds, sprouting and blossoming into the circumstances and situations that make up your life.

Gratitude is forcefully bound to your emotions. Like a tiny seed, gratitude will take root and eventually blossom into the events, environments, and occurrences that make up your daily life. The fruits of gratitude are opportunity and abundance.

An Extract from *29 Principles and Powers of Attraction* by Steven Claysen

Gem # Four:
The 'As If' Principle

When it comes to the Law of Attraction, it really is the thought that counts. Our greatest strength lies in the creative powers of the mind. The mind is like a garden. We either cultivate useful, beautiful plants (thoughts) purposely or we allow negative, destructive plants to thrive there by default.

Harvard psychologist, William James, developed what he has called the 'as if' principle. The 'as if' principle states that if we wish to possess something, an emotion, a qualification, a lifestyle, etc., we should act 'as if' we already had it. We should let it get a hold on us. We need to let it possess us. We must infuse our minds with the thought that we already have it. As Shakespeare said: "Assume a virtue if you have it not." No one has ever determined just how far the mind can go in shaping our circumstances.

Every thought we think has an impact on our personality and, consequently, on our success or failure at achieving the things we desire. When we express these thoughts in words, we significantly increase the force and power of our thinking. We are, ultimately, what we believe and feel. King Solomon wrote that we are what we think in our hearts. People can make themselves sick simply by thinking that they are sick. Wouldn't it also be true that we could make ourselves healthy by thinking healthy thoughts, or wealthy by thinking prosperous thoughts, or confident by thinking confidently about ourselves?

The British Army once tested the power of thinking on three individuals. They selected three men to determine the power of mental attitude on physical performance. The strength of these men was tested using a simple gripping device. Under normal circumstances, the three men had a gripping strength of about 100 pounds. When a scientist put them under hypnosis and made them believe that they were very weak, their best effort only registered an average of 39 pounds. Still under hypnosis, the scientist told the three men that they were extraordinarily strong. Their average grip rose to 142 pounds. When these men believed in themselves, their strength increased by nearly 300% over when they thought they were weak.

James Allen tells us that we hold "the key to every situation" and we contain the "transforming and re-generative agency" by which we make ourselves into whatever we desire. [14] It is significantly important what and how we think! The power of suggestion is tremendous.

To gain anything in life, we should cultivate and think and act the things we would like to be. When we have the energy to choose our own fate, we can obtain any desire we have in life if we pursue it. Arthur Simons wrote that "there is no dream that may not come true."

In *The Lehrman Project*, I wrote of a concept known as Tabula Rasa. In that particular section of the book, I mention that "when you believe something to be true, it becomes true for you, no matter what the facts may indicate to the contrary. Everything we are today is the result of an idea or an impression we took in and accepted as true. When we change the way we think and feel about ourselves and our world, then the world around us changes." [15]

The largest ocean cannot sink even the smallest ship unless the water gets inside it.

Allowing negative thinking into our mind is no different than poisoning our own drinking water. It is destructive and dangerous. When weak, negative, destroying thoughts get into our insides, we are in trouble and sinking fast. It is mental suicide.

William James explains that "if you form a picture in your mind of what you would like to be, and you keep and hold that picture there long enough, you will soon become exactly as you have been thinking."

The best road to success in any endeavor is to dream big, think big and give substance to your thoughts by acting big, by acting 'as if'. When our actions and attitudes reflect our passions and desires, we saturate ourselves with the power of attraction and then nothing can be withheld from us.

This is the 'as if' principle.

9 798822 400382 2